MW01628744

Love and thanks to my family and friends for their encouragement and support of my second book. To my daughters Jennifer and Emily, thanks for helping me see nature through your eyes. To my sister Karen, my wingman at signings, thanks for your great advice and excellent editing skills.

And to my husband Norman, who grew up in Miami and is my resource on the Florida environment, thank you for your unwavering support and Everglades insight. I love our hikes in this fascinating place and will never forget crossing paths with that bear.

Special thanks to the afterschool program at the Golisano Children's Museum of Naples (C'mon). Beth Housewert and her wonderful students were a tremendous source of inspiration and ideas for *E is for Everglades*.

I am honored that so many of you enjoyed *N is for Naples* and eagerly awaited this next book. Here it is. Enjoy!

-L.T.

E is for Everglades

PRT0915B

Printed in the United States.

ISBN-13: 9781620864418
ISBN-10: 162086441X

www.mascotbooks.com

E IS FOR EVERGLADES
WISH YOU WERE HERE!
GREETINGS FROM THE
EVERGLADES!
Lisa Trebilcock
Illustrated by
Cheri Nowak

A is for Airboat
Skims the water so fast
Seems to glide on air
Spot an alligator, at last!

is for Birds
Hundreds of species live here
Egrets, herons, bald eagles
Eat plenty of fish all year.

is for Cottonmouth
He's a dangerous brown snake
His bite is very venomous
Avoid him, for goodness sake!

is for Deer
Grazing in the sawgrass
Spotted fawns stay hidden
Waiting for dangers to pass.

is for Everglades
Its national park is ranked third
Of the largest parks in America
Perhaps you've already heard.

is for Fishing
Offers the best in the state
Snook, tarpon and bass
Hey, a gar just took my bait!

is for 'Gator
He glides quietly by
Look, he just spotted us
With beady little eyes.

is for Hardwood Hammock
High land that stays so dry
Mahogany, pine and palm trees
Seem to grow up to the sky.

is for Islands
Ten thousand, to be exact
That's a lot of islands
So many, it's a fact.

is for Junior Ranger
Fun program for girls and boys
Learn to protect the Everglades
For all of us to enjoy.

is for Kite
Swallowtail or snail
Both are large birds of prey
Only one has a forked tail.

is for Landscape
So unique and full of beauty
A subtropical wonder
Protecting it is our duty.

is for Mangroves
Thick near the shore
Their tangled roots are home
To crabs and fish galore!

is for Native Americans
Their legacies and pride stand strong
Calusa, Seminole, Miccosukee
Tribal traditions here run long.

O
is for Orchids
Plants so beautiful and rare
Like the elusive ghost bloom
Try to find one, if you dare.

is for Panther
Beautiful cat so hard to see
Prowls the Everglades at night
She climbs silently up a tree.

is for Question
How big is this place?
Nearly two million acres
I see the surprise on your face!

GULF OF MEXICO

THE EVERGLADES

ATLANTIC OCEAN

is for River
Waters flow gently, clear as glass
Author Marjory Stoneman Douglas
Called the Everglades a River of Grass.

is for Swamp Safari
Adventure out in your canoes
Hike through cypress forests
Wear your waterproof shoes.

is for Trail
Connects Tampa to Miami
When it opened in 1928
They named it the Tamiami.

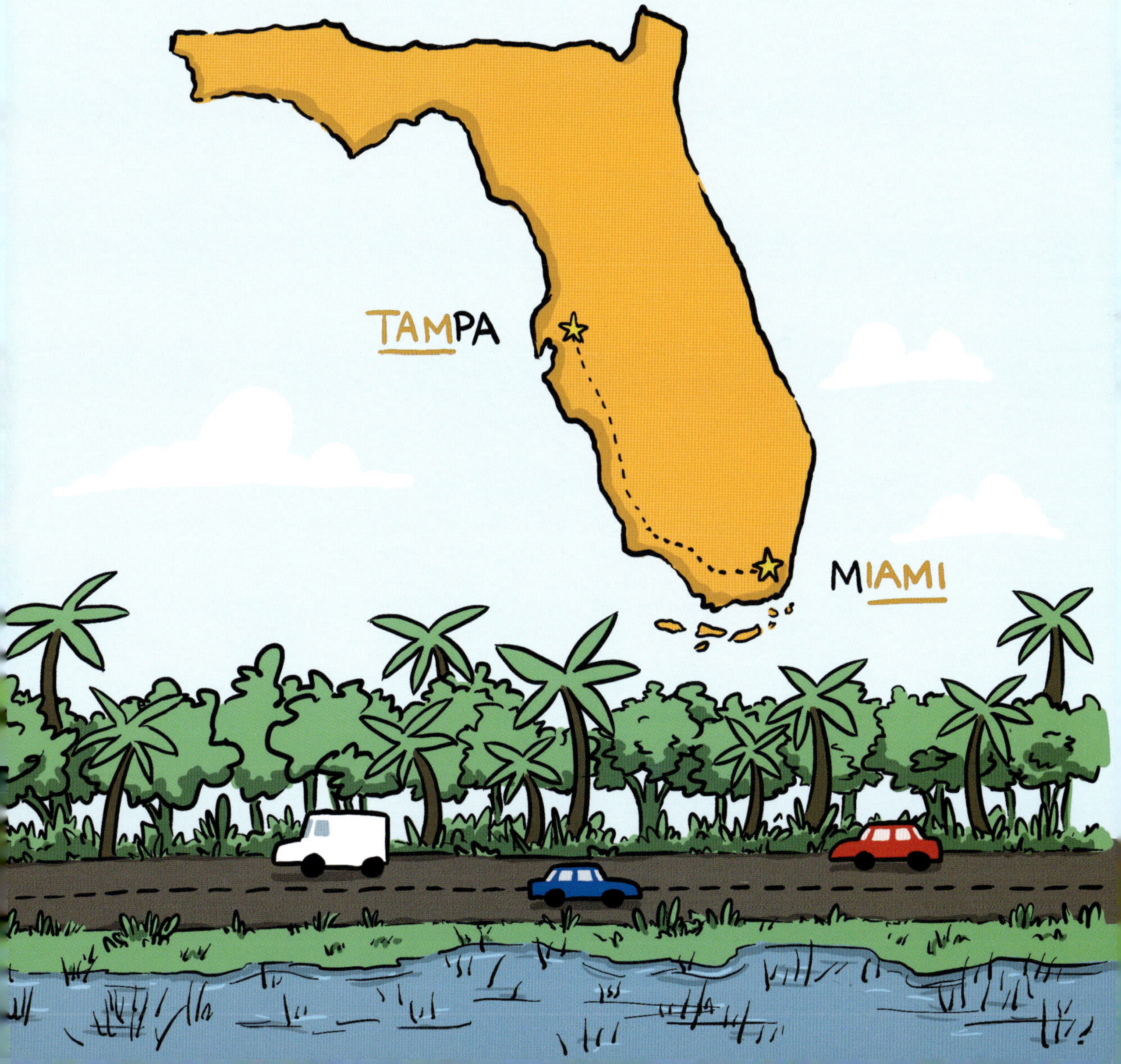

TAMPA

MIAMI

is for Unique
This ecological treasure
Wetlands and habitats so valuable
Their worth is beyond measure.

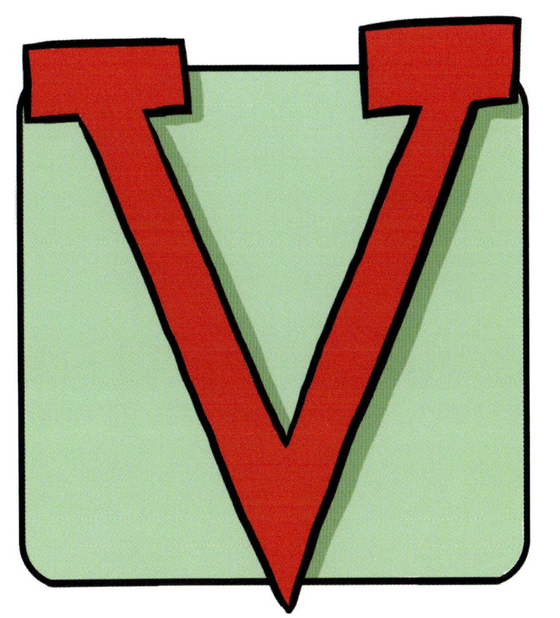

is for Visitors
So eager to explore
All the Everglades has to offer
Camping, biking, boating and more!

W is for Wildlife
This sanctuary is their home
Otters, bears and bobcats
Enjoy so much room to roam.

is for eXotics
Life that didn't start out here
Burmese pythons are an example
And cause a lot of fear.

is for You
Learning lots of information
All about the Everglades
Full of wonder and fascination.

is for Zig Zag
Run away from that 'gator!
Wait, he's only waving goodbye
And that he'll see you later!

The End

What have you seen in the Everglades?

When you see it, check it off.

- [ ] Mangrove
- [ ] Orchid
- [ ] Ranger
- [ ] Tent
- [ ] Wildlife

Lisa Trebilcock:

Lisa moved to Naples, Florida, in 1990, leaving cold New England winters behind. Born and raised in Connecticut, Lisa holds a Bachelor's degree in Journalism from Northeastern University in Boston and spent many years working in corporate marketing. Lisa has been honored by the School District of Collier County for over 3,500 volunteer hours. She and her husband, Norman, have two daughters, Jennifer and Emily. Their life in Naples is what inspired Lisa to write her first book, *N is for Naples,* and now *E is for Everglades.*

Cheri Nowak:

Cheri studied cartooning and illustration at the School of Visual Arts in New York City and Communication Design at the Fashion Institute of Technology. She's lived on Long Island her entire life and loves being close to both the beach and the city. Besides drawing, she enjoys sci-fi, reading, cake decorating, movies and spending time with her friends and family.